CONQUERING STRESS

BEFORE IT CONQUERS YOU

CONQUERING STRESS

BEFORE IT CONQUERS YOU

BILL RUDGE

LIVING TRUTH
PUBLISHERS
A DIVISION OF BILL RUDGE MINISTRIES, INC.
Hermitage, Pennsylvania

Unless otherwise indicated, Scripture quotations are from the New American Standard Bible, copyright © 1960, 1962, 1963, 1968, 1971, 1972, 1973, 1975, 1977, 1995 or 2020 by The Lockman Foundation. Used by permission. (Emphases added to Scriptures are by the author.)

Scripture quotations marked NKJV are from the New King James Version of the Bible, copyright © 1979, 1980, 1982 by Thomas Nelson, Inc.

Conquering Stress Before It Conquers You

Copyright © 1992 by Bill Rudge

Updated and expanded edition copyright © 2023 by Bill Rudge

ISBN 978-1-889809-12-0

Published by Living Truth Publishers
A Division of Bill Rudge Ministries, Inc.
Hermitage, Pennsylvania

www.billrudge.org

Typesetting by Pine Hill Graphics
Cover Design by Alpha Advertising

All rights reserved. No part of this publication may be reproduced, stored in a retrieval system or transmitted in any form by any means, electronic, mechanical, photocopy, recording, or otherwise, without prior permission of the author or publisher, except as provided by USA copyright law.

Produced in the United States of America.

CONTENTS

Today Is the Day 7

Adverse Effects of Stress. 9

Positive Stress. 11

How You Respond. 13

Fast-Paced Life and Ministry. 17

Be Realistic and Use Common Sense. 21

Organize and Reduce Clutter 25

Balance 27

Nutrition and Diet 29

Exercise. 31

Mental Attitude and Forgiveness 35

Overcoming Worry and Fear. 39

Rest, Relaxation and Recreation 43

Waiting on the Lord 47

Bible Study and Prayer 51

Right Relationship. 53

Hope During Times of Trouble. 57

Eternal Life. 61

For More Information 63

Chapter 3: What Happened During the Construction of the Erie Canal?

The Erie Canal wasn't the first attempt to build a waterway for transportation in the United States. In fact, George Washington himself was one of the biggest believers in a new canal. What's more, several significant cities along the Atlantic Ocean realized how valuable it would make them if the canal was to lead to their city. In Maryland, near George Washington's home and near the White House, a construction on a canal began in 1785. Washington said: "The way is easy and dictated by our clearest interest. It is to open a wide door, and make a smooth way for the produce of that Country to pass to our Markets ...."[5]

Called the Patowmack Canal, the point would be to connect the Potomac River all the way to the Ohio River Valley. However, after Washington's death in 1797, construction stopped on the canal. While a mile long portion of it had been built and it helped goods get past some dangerous rapids on the Potomac, the goal of reaching the Ohio River Valley was never reached.

In 1805, a flour merchant who had to deal every day with supply problems began to take it upon himself to build the canal. Named Jesse Hawley, he eventually convinced the Governor of New York, DeWitt Clinton, to build a canal between Lake Erie and Albany. The Governor went before the State Legislature and convinced them to give him the $7 million needed to build the Erie Canal.

---

[5] Quote source: http://www.nps.gov/grfa/historyculture/canal.htm

Today Is the Day

Tension levels mount as the pressures and stresses of life increase in both intensity and frequency. Countless people are experiencing chronic, sometimes acute anxiety in this hurried, oftentimes chaotic world with unfortunate repercussions.

Conflicts among families and friends, declining health, escalating medical expenses, shortages of services and supplies, occupational and financial difficulties, distressing news, disturbing images through the media, deteriorating moral standards, increasing spiritual deception, erratic behavior, strange phenomena, extreme weather conditions, environmental and electronic pollution, worldwide epidemics and famine, rampant violence, threats of nuclear war and other potentially cataclysmic events are causing inner turmoil and tension for earth's population. No wonder Jesus said regarding the *last* of the *last days*: "people fainting from fear and the expectation of the things that are coming upon the world" (Luke 21:26).

Perhaps you do not believe we are living during the prophesied end times and drawing nearer to the return of Jesus Christ. I am convinced you will soon. Nevertheless, even if you think the earth is merely going through another cycle that will eventually correct itself, or that the parallel occurrences of events today with those which are foretold in the Bible are just coincidences, this booklet will provide practical principles for helping you conquer the daily stresses of life—before they conquer you.

You need your health—physically, mentally, emotionally and above all spiritually—to adequately deal with life's challenges. Possessing wisdom, using common sense and living by biblical principles regarding the well-being of your body, mind and spirit will prove crucial.

Today is the day to begin learning how to successfully manage stress. My goal is to not merely prepare you to cope with the heightening pressures you face, but to inspire you to live victoriously amid them.

Adverse Effects of Stress

Many studies have been conducted and articles written that reveal the detrimental effects stress can have on our health and well-being. Excessive stress lowers our resistance to infection, weakens our natural defense system and makes us more vulnerable to sickness and disease. Research indicates that many symptoms and conditions can be related to, or exacerbated by, stress: tension headaches, indigestion, upset stomach, skin conditions, aches and pains, elevated blood pressure, heart palpitations, chest pain, diabetes, cancer, sleep problems, depression, anxiety, irritability, difficulty concentrating, or making decisions. (If you are having any of these or other adverse symptoms be sure to contact your health care provider.)

There is little doubt that major stress-provoking events in our lives can, and do, make us sick. But so can the *little* things—especially when they are ongoing, repetitive or occurring simultaneously.

Dr. Richard H. Dominguez, M.D., states in his book, *The Gift Of Health*:

> Colitis, ulcers, eczema, asthma, headaches, high blood pressure and its resultant stroke, kidney failure, heart attack or premature aging—all of these are caused to a varying degree by stress. Physicians use the term "target organ." The target organ is different in each of us. For some it is blood pressure, for others it is the colon or stomach or head or skin. How we handle stress hits us in our target organ.... Stress is one of the major things that makes us sick.

Positive Stress

It is impossible to avoid all stress. Besides, not all stress is harmful or unpleasant. In fact, life without some stress would be boring. What may be a negative and undesirable stress to one person may be a positive and likable stress to someone else. An individual who is afraid of heights would be terrified and experience severe stress if riding a chairlift up a mountainside, while a person who likes high places would enjoy the beautiful scenery and exhilarating ride.

The stress of walking to your car in a dark parking lot on a college campus or shopping center is actually a positive stress because it alerts you to be aware of your surroundings or causes you to have a security attendant accompany you. The tension an athlete faces before a contest motivates him or her not to take the event or their opponent for granted. It is preliminary stress and a desire to excel that inspires a singer or speaker to be prepared by rehearsing and practicing.

In all types of activities we incur stress. Some of it is beneficial. For example, when we exercise we are stressing our muscles. Without some resistance our muscles would become weak and atrophy. In the same way, the stresses of life are not always damaging—unless they are too severe, last too long, recur too frequently or are not alternated with periods of respite. This kind of stress and the continual "little hassles" of life accumulate to put our bodies and minds under excessive physical and emotional pressure. This is when stress becomes distress.

How You Respond

While you cannot control everything that happens in your life, you can control how you respond. Equally important in determining the effect stress has upon you is your response to it.

The desire to triumph over stress motivates me to respond in affirmative ways such as:

- having goals to keep focused in the right direction

- striving for excellence in everything I do so as not to have later regrets

- being organized and clutter free to lessen wasted time

- spending quality time in prayer and biblical study to renew my mind and refresh my spirit

- memorizing Scripture to counter the enemy's fiery darts

- relinquishing all my problems and hurts to the Lord

- trusting God to protect and provide for upcoming ventures

- taking "oasis breaks" with my wife and grandchildren

- eating nutritiously, exercising regularly and

- keeping a positive attitude.

A comfortable walk or conversation with a consoling friend can help unburden a heavy heart. Slow, gentle stretching helps alleviate pain. Exercise releases endorphins, which are chemicals produced naturally by the nervous system to cope with pain or stress and increase feelings of well-being. A cheerful smile, hearty laugh or encouraging word can lift your spirit or that of another.

There are certain people and circumstances that waste your time, drain your energy, create needless problems and turmoil, or divert you from doing God's will. You must

How You Respond

either avoid them or neutralize their influence. Wisdom of whom to (and whom not to) spend time with, and what to (and what not to) spend time doing, watching, reading and listening to is crucial. Feeling victimized and out-of-control must be negated. As much as possible, I avoid people and circumstances like that or limit them. When they cannot be avoided, I ask the Lord for wisdom and love concerning how to deal with them.

Being overwhelmed with negative or tragic news stories, world events and social media gossip can increase stress levels and wear you down. You can remain informed about important events but lessen the stress and anxiety by taking breaks from the media. Turn off your television, shut down your computer, silence your cell phone, refrain from continually checking news headlines and stop all social media for extended periods to spend quality time with loved ones and friends. Doing so will refresh and rejuvenate you. Removing secular television from my home over 20 years ago has proven to be a tremendous blessing in many ways and has lessened the stress in my life and family. Instead, my wife loves to watch inspirational Christian movies.

As much as possible I stay away from negative and pessimistic people (unless witnessing to them), limit their influence or ask the Lord for wisdom regarding how to deal with them. This enables me to gain control over my reactions so that I do not allow bitterness to take root in my heart. In prolonged or inescapable circumstances with cynical people who are constantly complaining or continually making cruel comments, I strive to consider their motives instead of their behavior and find an opportunity to reach them with the Gospel. Perhaps, God is using them and the circumstances to help me develop more patience, love and self-control. Either way, I know the Lord has a purpose for all things that enter and affect my life. Therein lies peace during difficult circumstances or dealing with negative people.

Fast-Paced Life and Ministry

Life for me has often been hectic. My wife, Karen, and I raised two children who were engaged in a variety of activities. We often had temporary foster children as well as family members and guests staying with us for extended periods of time. Then came eleven wonderful, energetic grandchildren. I often tell people that each one of my grandchildren has an MD degree. As they look at me in bewilderment because of their young ages, I explain that their MD degree stands for Major Distraction. However, that Major Distraction is what I consider a blessed "oasis" and a much-needed break from oftentimes incessant work. Besides, they are potential future staff for a ministry or church because they have helped in a diversity of ways at this ministry. As I did with my children, I seek to impart life-lessons and faith into their lives. I never consider them an intrusion, but an opportunity and a blessing.

For over 45 years I have directed this multifaceted ministry consisting of such activities as: speaking engagements in churches and schools in the U.S. and abroad, coordinating and leading mission trips and Holy Land Adventures, organizing area-wide events, coaching soccer, teaching exercise and self-defense classes, leading groups through our obstacle course, producing radio broadcasts, writing newsletters and books, maintaining a website and other responsibilities that are part of a growing international outreach. In addition, much time and energy has been spent conducting research and investigation, as well as serving as chaplain in stressful situations of crisis intervention.

My life and interests revolve around four main things: the Lord, family, ministry and health. Little else distracts or diverts me for very long as I strive to stay focused on the priorities the Lord has given me. Early mornings and late evenings (sometimes in the middle of the night) supply adequate time for me to fulfill ministry deadlines and still have quality family time. Working longer hours September through May enables me to rejuvenate during the summer months, spending extra time working outside at the ministry center, running obstacle courses, traveling, speaking and doing various activities with the grandchildren.

Occasionally I have tried to slow life down, but usually to no avail. It only seems to accelerate. So, I have learned to accept busyness as a normal way of life for me. Somehow, God has supplied the needed time and energy to continue such a pace. He has bestowed His peace in the middle of distressing circumstances. Nonetheless, being aware that nonstop activities are notorious for burnout and health decline encourages me to compensate by still being disciplined in virtually every area of my life.

Like an athlete preparing for his next contest, I discipline myself and am constantly training (exercising, eating nutritionally, fasting, praying, studying Scripture and so on) to better handle the daily stresses of life, to be able to fulfill an oftentimes rigorous ministry schedule, to be prepared for the rigors of my next mission adventure, to participate in physical activities with my grandchildren and to be a more effective witness for

Christ. The goal is to maintain my health and vitality to fulfill God's purpose and finish the race He has called me to run.

Without being refreshed through prayer and fasting, renewing my mind with God's Word and periods of relaxation, I would have nothing to offer those seeking my help.

Be Realistic and Use Common Sense

An important principle in reducing stress is to be realistic. Scripture has taught me many great lessons about reducing stress and maximizing effectiveness through delegation. Like Moses, I discovered I could not do it all alone. Moses sat as judge for the children of Israel from morning to evening. When Moses' father-in-law, Jethro, saw this, he admonished Moses, "The thing that you are doing is not good. You will surely wear out, both yourself and these people who are with you, for the task is too heavy for you; you cannot do it alone" (Exodus 18:17-18). Jethro advised Moses to select able helpers and delegate to them much of the responsibility that his son-in-law had previously been assuming. Moses followed his wise counsel (Exodus 18:19-26).

Early on I realized that I could not achieve the goals and vision the Lord placed on my heart without help. So, I trained volunteers and then delegated various responsibilities to them. Doing so multiplied my time and maximized ministry effectiveness. We also developed a referral ministry for those needing specialized help or counseling.

As the ministry continued to grow, an endless stream of people were coming to ask for my help and advice. As I sought the Lord concerning this, He impressed on my heart to focus on speaking engagements, radio broadcasts, authoring books and pamphlets and producing audio messages. This multiplied the ministry outreaches from touching hundreds of lives to having an impact on thousands—not just in our local area, but across the U.S. and around the world.

Initially I tried to accept every ministry opportunity, but I quickly realized the impossibility of that and learned to say, "No." The Lord has given me clear instruction not to be diverted, no matter how good the cause, from fulfilling the primary focus, specific goals and vision He has for my life and ministry.

Be Realistic and Use Common Sense

It is better to limit your involvements and be more effective, than to be spread so thin that you become ineffective. In life and ministry, it is advantageous to do *less* better than to do *more* poorly. Do not rush through something and do it shoddily. You will be disappointed with the outcome and probably have to redo it sooner than you would like. In my estimation, *quality* is more important than *quantity*. In all you do, strive for excellence.

The ministry's radio studio engineer told me to never buy cheap equipment because in the end it would cost more in both money and time for needed repairs and frequent replacement. His sage advice proved true. The radio equipment operated efficiently the entire life of our production studio.

Waiting until the last minute to fulfill important responsibilities often leads to frantic behavior which causes mistakes and increases stress. I know. I used to exist on adrenaline because I enjoyed living on the edge and waited until the last possible minute to fulfill deadlines. Although I performed well under pressure, and often had no alternative, it takes its toll on health. Wisdom dictates, when at all possible, complete your deadline projects ahead of time. It will remove much of the unnecessary pressure and stress, and you will enjoy peace of mind.

Many people have good goals and intentions, but get sidetracked, wasting too much time on secondary issues, while the priorities God has called them to are neglected. They squander valuable time and energy by *majoring* in nonessentials (mundane activities with no eternal value) while *minoring* in what are the real essentials (that which is of utmost importance). You know exactly what I am talking about. Step back and evaluate the focus of your life. Make the necessary adjustments to get your priorities straight.

Organize and Reduce Clutter

Years ago, I read in *The Legal Alert* magazine that, "Pastors are less likely to experience a burnout syndrome when they are more organized and more disciplined in their schedules. Time management is critical."

I too have learned that being organized, disciplined and having good time management skills (while remaining sensitive to the spontaneous leading of the Holy Spirit and responding to unexpected needs) are beneficial in that not only are the pressures lessened, but much more is accomplished. A cluttered and disorganized home or workplace not only wastes time and energy looking for things, but it often creates internal stress and anxiety which can cause mistakes—some that could even prove fatal to yourself or others. Therefore, lessen stress by decluttering and organizing.

While I am usually organized and do not like disorder, things have a way of accumulating. Consequently, every so often I go through my entire house, garage, office and ministry center (checking drawers, cabinets, shelves, closets and the like) to give away books, equipment, supplies, clothes and other things that may better serve someone else. This always proves to be a tremendous de-stressing strategy. The weight on my back and shoulders seems lighter. My mind seems clearer. My home and ministry center become more peaceful.

Less sometimes is *better*. Less clutter results in less stress and more efficiency. Less waste supplies more resources. Less negative thinking brings a better attitude and nurtures emotional stability. Less criticism generates better friendships. Less worry and fear improves overall well-being. Less junk food produces better health. Less financial debt (and not paying interest) enhances financial security. Less bickering creates more peace in the home. Less contending with the Lord makes one more productive in ministry.

Balance

There is an interrelationship between physical, emotional and spiritual stress. Therefore, to reduce and effectively deal with the stress in our lives, we must deal with each of these areas. As we obey the instructions in God's Guide Book (the Bible) and apply the biblical health principles through proper nutrition, regular exercise, adequate rest and relaxation, a good mental attitude and a personal trust in Jesus Christ, we will inevitably be better off in body, mind and spirit.

Physically, our bodies are the temples of the Holy Spirit and should be "living sacrifices"—totally committed to the Lord in every aspect for His honor and glory. Mentally, we are to be transformed by the renewing of our minds. Emotionally, we must not allow negative and destructive feelings such as worry, fear, jealousy, bitterness, hate, revenge, greed, impatience and pride to dominate our lives. Instead, they must be replaced with the fruit of the Spirit: love, joy, peace, patience, kindness, goodness, faithfulness, gentleness and self-control. Spiritually, we are created in God's image and are to be conformed to the image of Jesus Christ, filled with and led by the Holy Spirit.

To violate or disregard the wisdom inherent in the natural health laws established by God would cause one needless stress and resultant maladies. This is one reason why many are in poor condition and do not achieve the full purpose God has for them. It is sad indeed that many believers in Christ who have such a strong desire to serve the Lord are unable to effectively do so because they lack the necessary health and energy.

When someone is in pain, stress intensifies and efficacy lessens. Pain—whether physical or emotional—needs to be alleviated through exercise, nutrition, relaxation and other natural and safe methods so as not to incur negative side effects. And don't forget the amazing benefits of prayer, "meditating" on God's Word, Scripture memorization and fellowship with other believers.

Nutrition and Diet

Our diet is an important factor regarding overcoming stress and achieving optimal health. Many of the foods we eat are refined, with much of the natural vitamins, minerals, enzymes and other essential nutrients depleted, while many undesirable ingredients and chemicals have been added. Excessive consumption of devitalized food makes us vulnerable to depression and sickness and robs us of vitality and energy.

When I ate mostly refined, cooked and devitalized foods containing lots of unhealthy fats, artificial sweeteners, salt, white flour and chemical additives, I experienced fatigue and was less able to handle stressful situations. But now that I eat more naturally: mostly fresh fruits and vegetables, raw nuts and seeds, natural whole grains, and other nutritious foods, and drink plenty of pure water and fruit and vegetable juices, I feel better and am able to more effectively deal with and overcome the pressures in my life. Also, I have more energy and vitality for the ministry to which God has called me.

I have discovered that eating healthy foods as close as possible to the way God gave them in nature—before being inappropriately modified, refined, over-cooked and filled with artificial colors, preservatives, sweeteners and so forth—is usually the best principle to follow. The resulting improved digestion, assimilation and elimination are crucial to maintain one's health and overcome stress.

Exercise

Exercise is something else I do to relieve stress and keep in shape. Tests have revealed that those who do not get adequate exercise are less capable of withstanding stress than those who do. Increasing flexibility, strength and endurance through a regular and reasonable exercise program is an excellent way to endure times of excessive stress. Tension negatively affects the nervous system, and when muscles are exercised, the nervous system relaxes. Going to bed tired from nervous fatigue makes it difficult to sleep. But going to bed tired from muscle fatigue induces sleep.

Walking is still one of the best forms of exercise and, as a natural tranquilizer, it is calming, relaxing and even uplifting. In Bible days, people walked everywhere so they did not need additional forms of exercise like we do because of our sedentary lifestyle. Walking with my wife around the ministry property or in the park or walking alone prayerfully meditating on God's Word is a great stress reliever. In fact, it makes me feel better than other stress reducing techniques I have tried—except perhaps reclining in my hammock on a balmy summer day.

It does not matter how old you are or what shape you may be in, it's never too late to begin taking care of your body, the temple of the Holy Spirit, and thereby glorify God. A Christian should not be excessively overweight and out of shape unless he or she has a physical disability or medical problem. We, of all people, should be the example, not only spiritually, but also physically.

Motivation, commitment, determination, discipline and dedication are important elements for a successful fitness program. Taking proper care of your miraculous body, the temple of the Holy Spirit, will provide numerous health benefits such as having more energy, feeling and looking better, being less prone to injury, dealing with stress more effectively and having a better, more confident attitude. Your goal should not just be to get in shape, but to maintain the best condition possible by making health and fitness a lifetime commitment.

Dr. Hyder, M.D., writes in his book *Shape Up*:

> The words *soma* and *sarx* in the New Testament Greek, usually translated body and flesh, respectively, are not synonymous. *Body* means the physical temple, a creation of God, not in itself implicated in moral issues. *Flesh*, by contrast, does have a moral connotation. It is used in the description of those thoughts and activities of the body which are contrary to the influence of the Spirit of God within it. We have, therefore, a responsibility to take care of the body (*soma*), to keep it healthy, and to use it in accordance with God's will, led by the Spirit, resisting the flesh (*sarx*).

My specially designed 30 to 60 minute workouts (consisting of stretching, flexibility, balance, strengthening and endurance exercises) that I do four to six days a week are tremendously helpful. Not only does my exercise time enable me to get away from all the hassles and pressures in life, but after a vigorous workout, I feel refreshed, energetic and more determined in my work for the Lord.

Some people tell me they do not have time to exercise, but I reply that I do not have time *not* to exercise. The physical, mental, emotional and even spiritual benefits make these few hours a week a wise and necessary investment. It always seems to increase my focus and energy to accomplish more throughout the day.

(For additional insight on physical, mental, emotional and spiritual health, see two other books I have written entitled *Reaching Your Maximum Potential in Christ* and *Fasting for Sensitivity and Power*.)

Mental Attitude and Forgiveness

Since there is no way to avoid all the pressure and stress in our lives, we must learn to victoriously live with them. Instead of allowing stress to victimize us, we can control our attitudes and emotions in the midst of life's stress-producing circumstances. The amount of stress is usually not as crucial as the manner in which we handle it.

Research indicates the mind (*psyche*) produces various changes in the body (*soma*), thus the term psychosomatic. Allowing negative and destructive emotions such as jealousy, envy, anger, resentment, vengeance, self-pity, fear and hopelessness to linger can do great harm to the physical body and result in a host of psychosomatic diseases. I sometimes demonstrate the effects of these damaging emotions by telling people to make a fist, squeeze it as tight as possible and hold it tightly for as long as they can. Then I tell them, "This is what prolonged anger, hatred and unforgiveness do to you. Forgiveness," I explain "is like releasing your tightened fist; it lets go of your emotional burdens."

No wonder Jesus said to forgive others. He knew the destructive nature of unrelenting hate and anger and the healing benefit of love and forgiveness. Besides, how can we expect God to forgive us if we do not forgive others (Matthew 6:14-15)? Jesus said to forgive up to seventy times seven (Matthew 18:22). Following His advice not only benefits our spiritual life but can also save us from many unwanted ailments.

Our attitude is one of the most important aspects in overcoming the adverse effects of stress. We need to continually seek to have the attitude of the psalmist, "This is the day which the LORD has made; let us rejoice and be glad in it" (Psalm 118:24).

If negative thoughts and attitudes creep up on you, emotions can speedily spiral downward. It is easy for discouragement, frustration and feelings of helplessness and hopelessness to ensue. However, as soon as you make an attitude adjustment of faith and confidence in the Lord, your perspective will radically change, and many times your circumstances will also improve.

When you "rejoice in the Lord always" (Philippians 4:4) and "in everything give thanks" (1 Thessalonians 5:18), then you will discover that "the joy of the LORD is your strength" (Nehemiah 8:10). Proverbs 17:22 states, "A joyful [glad, merry, cheerful] heart is good medicine [causes good healing], but a broken spirit dries up the bones."

"A tranquil heart is life to the body, but jealousy is rottenness to the bones" (Proverbs 14:30). The contrast is clear: negativity and destructive emotions erode well-being, while positive emotions and attitudes benefit health.

Listening to praise music during stressful times changes my focus almost immediately and seems to transport my spirit into a peaceful dimension of God's presence. Praying, reflecting on God's Word, memorizing Scripture and worshiping the Lord are great antidotes for stressful times, creating internal peace no matter what the situation.

Philippians 4:8 gives a list of positive things which should fill the thought life of the believer: "whatever is true, whatever is honorable, whatever is right, whatever is pure, whatever is lovely [lovable and gracious], whatever is commendable, if there is any excellence and if anything worthy of praise, think about these things." For how we feel and the way we act is a direct result of what we think and dwell upon. When we persist in pleasant emotions such as love, forgiveness, joy, peace, hope and faith we induce good health.

Overcoming Worry and Fear

Worry and fear that immobilize you are destructive. But care and concern which motivate you to pray, trust in the Lord and take positive action are beneficial.

Isaiah 26:3 is of great encouragement. It says: "The steadfast of mind You will keep in perfect peace, because he trusts in You." The NKJV says it this way: "You will keep him in perfect peace, whose mind is stayed on You, because he trusts in You." Now let's reverse that verse and personalize it as follows: Because I trust in You my mind is stayed on You, therefore, You will keep me in perfect peace.

The one whose mind is "stayed" on television, movies, the Internet, talk radio ... is often stressed and depressed. But the person whose mind is focused on the Lord has peace—even when surrounded by difficult circumstances. The very next verse states: "Trust in the LORD forever, for in GOD the LORD, we have an everlasting Rock" (Isaiah 26:4). You can have peace *with* the Lord and also have the peace *of* the Lord, so let nothing alienate you from Him or steal the peace you have with Him.

Christ is our peace. His Word brings us peace. His presence brings us peace. The words of the apostle Paul in Philippians 4:4-7 are both an admonishment and an encouragement for all believers: "Rejoice in the Lord always; again I will say, rejoice! Let your gentle spirit be known to all men. The Lord is near. Be anxious for nothing, but in everything by prayer and supplication with thanksgiving let your requests be made known to God. And the peace of God, which surpasses all comprehension, will guard your hearts and your minds in Christ Jesus."

Dr. David Jeremiah insightfully stated, "Choosing to rejoice in the midst of stressful circumstances is not a normal reaction in our world. But it should be the Christian's response. We know the One who is sovereignly reigning over all the earth. Therefore, we can rejoice in any and all circumstances. We can say with the apostle Paul, 'Rejoice in the Lord always' (Philippians 4:4). Rejoice today, no matter what comes your way."

One of my prayers during an intense time of fasting and prayer every January is, "Lord, help me to overcome worry, doubt and unbelief through unwavering faith and trust in You. Help me to walk in Your peace and rest in You, knowing that You have it all in control and are working it out for good, and that the result will be ultimate victory." I also pray, "Lord, help me to conquer fear so that I fear no man, woman, beast, being or situation but only fear and reverence You and walk in Your courage, strength and power. Help me to trust You to defend me and fight my battles. Help me not to be a "people pleaser" but a "God fearer" and help me to care more about Your opinion than people's. The only opinion that really matters is Yours—You are the One I stand before to give an account of my life."

Rest, Relaxation and Recreation

Another key to overcoming stress and having a healthy lifestyle is rest, relaxation and recreation. As well as needing proper sleep, some leisure is not a waste of time or a misuse of talent.

It is true that we are living in the end times and prophetic indicators declare that Christ's coming is rapidly approaching. You may feel an urgency, like me, to work while we still have the opportunity. Jesus said concerning His own time of ministry on earth, "We must work the works of Him who sent Me as long as it is day; night is coming when no one can work" (John 9:4). How much more true is this for us today? Even so, we should follow the example of our Creator who rested on the seventh day following creation. He instructs us to do likewise. Those who rest one day a week from their labors are usually healthier, happier and more productive than those who fail to follow God's example.

In Mark 6:30-32 we read: "The apostles gathered together with Jesus; and they reported to Him all that they had done and taught. And He said to them, 'Come away by yourselves to a secluded place and rest a little while.' (For there were many people coming and going, and they did not even have time to eat.) And they went away in the boat to a secluded place by themselves."

While it is true that some people are downright lazy, other people feel needless guilt for taking any time for rest, relaxation and recreation. These are usually the very ones who push themselves until they have a physical or mental breakdown and are then "forced" to rest.

Many people, especially those in ministry, work long hours. The majority of pastors and ministry leaders thoroughly enjoy what they do, but they often neglect to follow the health principles in God's Word. Consequently, many eventually succumb to an unexpected health crisis or emotional problem that makes them slow down or stop altogether. I have talked with several ministers and Christian leaders who thought they were exempt because they were working for the Lord. Inevitably, they discover that God's natural health laws also apply to them regardless of faith or vocation.

A real challenge for me is to balance the diversity of ministry opportunities and responsibilities in light of the nearness of Jesus' return that I sense in my spirit, while not neglecting valuable time with the Lord or my wife, children and grandchildren. Besides, many of the illustrations for my messages and articles have come during times of relaxing and contemplating the Lord and His Word or through insight gained from being with family members and friends.

If we neglect time for rest, relaxation and recreation, we may temporarily accomplish a lot in our career but lose our health and family in the process. We must schedule some leisure time in our daily schedule. Occasionally escaping life's pressures with just some brief relief is like a mini-vacation. Take a few minutes when feeling overwhelmed to lie on some warm grass looking up at a gentle blue sky or relax comfortably on a recliner or lounge chair. One of my favorite methods of relaxation is on a beautiful Sunday afternoon in the summer, to stretch my hammock between two trees and just lay there relaxing, enjoying the gentle breeze and pondering the wonders of God and creation and the revelation of Jesus Christ in Scripture.

It is profitable to occasionally stop the hectic pace of life and allow time for something that will refresh, renew and rejuvenate your body, mind and spirit. We must understand that the body and brain (and the spirit I should say) function more effectively, and that we can do far more for the Lord, when we take time for rest, relaxation and recreation.

The psalmist did not need tranquilizers or sleeping pills for he said: "In peace I will both lie down and sleep, for You alone, O LORD, make me to dwell in safety" (Psalm 4:8). Oftentimes, as soon as my head hits the pillow, I fall into a naturally deep sleep—with many pleasant and interesting dreams. My body takes advantage of any opportunity to restore and revitalize. Like riding a bicycle, I am constantly moving (peddling) throughout the day and into the evening, but once I sit down (stop peddling) for long, I can quickly doze off into a deep, peaceful sleep. As long as I am peddling (moving) I stay up; once I stop peddling (sit down), I fall over (rest from exhaustion).

Waiting on the Lord

Jesus frequently got away to spend time alone with the Father (Matthew 14:23; Mark 1:35; 6:46; Luke 5:16; 6:12; 9:18). And we should do likewise.

As a young minister, I learned how important it is to take time to "wait on the Lord." One summer, I was guest speaker for a week at a nearby camp. I was commuting every day from the camp to my office to handle the regular ministry requirements. In addition to all that, we recently had 3.7 acres of land donated to our ministry, and I was needed to make decisions on the building design and materials, as well as help with the construction. Towards the end of that week, I was totally exhausted; every ounce of strength and energy was drained from me. While I believe in Philippians 4:13, "I can do all things through Him who strengthens me" and have literally *built* my life and ministry on this biblical truth, I had to honestly ask the Lord, "How can I now experience Your strength?"

Instantly, I was mindful of Isaiah 40:31: "Yet those who wait [hope in] for the LORD will gain new strength; they will mount up with wings like eagles, they will run and not get tired, they will walk and not become weary." Similarly, I discovered the wisdom of the psalmist: "I will lift up my eyes to the mountains; from where shall my help come? My help comes from the LORD, Who made heaven and earth" (Psalm 121:1-2).

That day I forgot about what I thought needed to be done and spent time alone with my Lord. I remembered how Jesus took time to get away and be alone with the Father. He was able to keep His composure and remain cool and calm, even when facing extreme pressure and opposition. The Lord also taught me that no matter how determined I was or how much self-discipline I had, I could never accomplish His purpose and goals for my life through my own strength and determination.

I realized that it is by God's Spirit, not through my might and power (Zechariah 4:6).

That evening I gave my final message at camp with renewed strength. The Lord's Spirit challenged the people as only He can, and in such a way that most of them spent more than an hour praying at the altar. Following that, I shared with many on a one-to-one basis, yet my mind remained fresh and alert. Truly, I had found a source of strength, "waiting on the Lord." Now I frequently separate myself from everything and everyone to spend time alone with the Lord.

As previously indicated, I am under continual time constraints and constant deadlines. Frequently we face financial pressures of a growing ministry, and I am called upon to provide crisis intervention for many individuals and families. The circumstances surrounding me are often chaotic and stressful—physically and mentally draining to say the least. Nevertheless, I have an internal peace and joy from trusting and resting in the Lord.

The difficulties and obstacles enveloping my life and ministry are overcome as I "strengthen" myself in the Lord as David did when his city was burned, the women and children taken captive and the people spoke of stoning him (1 Samuel 30:1-6).

Reflecting on God's past faithfulness during my life's journey and being encouraged with the remembrance of His many lessons and victories, have imparted to me "the peace of God, which surpasses all comprehension" (Philippians 4:7).

Life is not a 100-yard dash, but a marathon. You must pace yourself by spending time waiting on the Lord, cultivating relationships with family and friends and taking care of your overall health. Then, you will not spend yourself prematurely or look back upon your life with regret. That is why I pray and fast every January for one to three weeks and at other times throughout the year so that I can "wait upon the Lord" and seek Him with all my heart so as to have His priorities, presence and peace in my life.

Bible Study and Prayer

Taking time to read the Word and pray (albeit sometimes only briefly) three times a day—morning, noon, and evening has proven to be one of the most beneficial decisions I have ever made.

My Bible study format is as follows: When I begin a new book of the Bible, I enjoy getting some time alone and read the entire book straight through or listen to it on an audio recording to get an overview of it. Then I go back and re-read it chapter by chapter and contemplate its meaning. I meditate on each verse, like a cow chewing its cud, trying to assimilate it into my spiritual lifeblood.

During this second reading, I do background research, examine corresponding Scripture references and sometimes use a commentary or other reference material. It might take me a month or more to go through one book of the Bible in this manner. Then I re-read the entire book straight through again. This is an effective way to learn and remember Scripture.

By following this procedure, God's truth and principles have come alive in my mind, my heart and my life. When I take time for Bible study and prayer, the Lord seems to multiply my time and the day usually goes much better for me—making the difficulties and deadlines much easier to deal with.

While walking with Karen near our ministry center or in the local park, we often quote Bible verses and pray together. I will say the first part of a verse then Karen will finish the rest of it. After quoting numerous scriptures we hold hands and pray while continuing our walk. This has been one of our favorite ways to relax, commit Scripture to memory and spend quality time together. It not only edifies us spiritually but reduces stress while providing physical and emotional benefits as well.

Right Relationship

We are living at a time when men and women's hearts are literally failing them because of fear. As a result, many people are turning to various New Age techniques and practices or succumbing to alcohol and drugs to cope with the escalating pressures. But there is a far better way. *Knowing* the Lord Jesus Christ and *living* according to biblical truth and principles are far superior to any other means or method for obtaining lasting inner peace and joy.

In trying to become more than they were created to be, equal with God, Adam and Eve (and thereby all their human offspring) became less than God initially intended them to be. Our insecurities and fears naturally occur because we inherently realize we are in a fallen state. So, we search and go on spiritual journeys in our quests to find something, anything, that we think is missing in our lives.

Maureen Bradley eloquently wrote, "God, our Creator, has formed man with not only a physical body, but within that magnificent body is an inner realm even more significant, glorious, and powerful.... This stately place, the soul of man, was designed for habitation by God and not for any other."

The achievement of a successful spiritual journey will elude us until we come to faith in Jesus Christ. He alone rightly guarantees a future hope of our mortal bodies being transformed into glorified bodies and all of creation being restored to its intended magnificence. When that final day of redemption comes—and it will—believers will dwell in God's visible presence for all eternity. Until then, be assured that our Creator who designed us knows what is best for our bodies, minds and spirits.

A most significant aspect of reducing and controlling stress in this life is being in a right relationship with the Creator. People who are still spiritually searching, living in rebellion before the Lord or attempting to earn salvation through their own efforts, usually have tremendous inner turmoil and tension, as do believers who are living in willful disobedience or know in their heart that something is not right between them and the Lord. The most important principle of health is to "Fear [reverence] the LORD and turn away from evil. It will be healing to your body and refreshment to your bones" (Proverbs 3:7-8).

Nothing is more fulfilling and peaceful than living in right relationship with the Creator. Honoring Him with your life and walking in obedience to His will provides an inner tranquility that transcends all circumstances. Amid difficulties and uncertainties you can be assured that everything is under control because God is working behind the scenes to accomplish His purpose and ultimately bring good to your life.

We will manage the stresses of life much better when we feel healthy physically, have a positive mental attitude and have a vibrant relationship with the Lord Jesus Christ. Knowing that our lives are in the center of God's will and trusting Him with everything that happens is the best antidote to triumph over the pressures and stresses of everyday life.

Hope During Times of Trouble

Through Christ we have available the strength to change those stresses that are unnecessary, accept those circumstances we cannot change, control emotions that are not beneficial, and maintain faith and a positive attitude—even in the midst of stressful situations. Receiving God's forgiveness and new life in Christ will not remove all our stress and pressure in this life, and in some ways may actually increase them, but it will provide an inner peace, joy and hope no matter what we encounter.

After his Damascus Road experience and becoming a committed believer in Jesus Christ, the apostle Paul faced many troubles and hardships: criticism, rejection, beatings, shipwrecks, imprisonment and more. God's grace was sufficient for Paul to not only endure these stresses, but to live victoriously in the midst of them. Paul states in 2 Corinthians 4:8-9, "we are afflicted in every way, but not crushed; perplexed, but not despairing; persecuted, but not forsaken; struck down, but not destroyed."

No influence or pressure could force Paul to give up in defeat or deny his faith in Christ. He wrote Philippians 4:11-13 from personal experience: "Not that I speak from want, for I have learned to be content in whatever circumstances I am. I know how to get along with humble means, and I also know how to live in prosperity; in any and every circumstance I have learned the secret of being filled and going hungry, both of having abundance and suffering need. I can do all things through Him who strengthens me."

The apostle Paul encourages all believers with the following inspiring words in his letter to the church in Rome: "Who will separate us from the love of Christ? Will tribulation, or distress, or persecution, or famine, or nakedness, or peril, or sword? But in all these things we overwhelmingly conquer through Him who loved us. For I am convinced that neither death, nor life, nor angels, nor principalities, nor things present, nor things to come, nor powers, nor height, nor depth, nor any other created thing, will be able to separate us from the love of God, which is in Christ Jesus our Lord" (Romans 8:35, 37-39).

The apostle Paul had a faith and hope in Christ that transcended the difficulties he faced in a fallen and hostile world. He confidently wrote, "...the time of my departure has come. I have fought the good fight, I have finished the course, I have kept the faith; in the future there is laid up for me the crown of righteousness, which the Lord, the righteous Judge, will award to me on that day; and not only to me, but also to all who have loved His appearing" (2 Timothy 4:6-8).

When our lives are in a right relationship with the Lord and we are living by the principles in His Word and walking in His peace and resting in Him, we can effectively deal with conditions that would otherwise devastate us. Psalm 46:1-2 states: "God is our refuge and strength, a very present help in trouble. Therefore we will not fear, though the earth should change and though the mountains slip into the heart of the sea."

Eternal Life

All of our good nutrition, exercise, positive mental attitude, rest, relaxation and recreation may help to alleviate stress, but they will never give us eternal life—unless we also come to know Jesus Christ as our Savior and Lord. Even more important than seeking to live a life of bliss is that we come to know the Author of abundant and eternal life (John 10:10). John 17:3 says: "This is eternal life, that they may know You, the only true God, and Jesus Christ whom You have sent."

Since the creation of Adam and Eve in the Garden of Eden, God has desired to be with His people in a paradise setting. His plan is to dwell with us forever so that we may behold His glory and be blessed by Him throughout eternity. In the words of the *Westminster Shorter Catechism*, "What is the chief end of man? Man's chief end is to glorify God, and to enjoy Him forever."

Through faith in Jesus Christ we can look forward with anticipation to our eventual physical, mental, emotional and spiritual perfection. "Beloved, now we are children of God, and it has not appeared as yet what we will be. We know that when He appears, we will be like Him, because we will see Him just as He is. And everyone who has this hope fixed on Him purifies himself, just as He is pure" (1 John 3:2-3).

Until that time when pain, suffering and death are forever eliminated, we can better serve and honor God here and now by conquering the stress that controls and impairs our lives. Doing so will give us increased energy and vitality for living and enable us to achieve the potential and purpose He has for each one of our lives.

Today is the day to begin a new life of "conquering stress before it conquers you!"

For More Information

Bill Rudge has produced numerous books, pamphlets and audio messages on a variety of timely topics. For a complete listing or a copy of his informative newsletter, visit www.billrudge.org or write to:

Bill Rudge Ministries
P.O. Box 108
Sharon, PA 16146
U.S.A.
www.billrudge.org

Notes